EMMANUEL JOSEPH

Crypto Waves: Riding the Highs and Lows of Digital Currency

Copyright © 2025 by Emmanuel Joseph

All rights reserved. No part of this publication may be reproduced, stored or transmitted in any form or by any means, electronic, mechanical, photocopying, recording, scanning, or otherwise without written permission from the publisher. It is illegal to copy this book, post it to a website, or distribute it by any other means without permission.

First edition

This book was professionally typeset on Reedsy. Find out more at reedsy.com

Contents

1	Chapter 1: The Dawn of Digital Currency	1
2	Chapter 2: The Rise of Altcoins	3
3	Chapter 3: The Bull Run and the Bubble	5
4	Chapter 4: Blockchain Beyond Currency	7
5	Chapter 5: The Regulatory Landscape	9
6	Chapter 6: The Role of Institutional Investors	11
7	Chapter 7: Decentralized Finance (DeFi) Revolution	13
8	Chapter 8: Non-Fungible Tokens (NFTs) and the Creative...	15
9	Chapter 9: Security and the Fight Against Fraud	17
10	Chapter 10: The Global Impact of Digital Currency	19
11	Chapter 11: The Future of Digital Currency	21
12	Chapter 12: Embracing the Crypto Wave	23

1

Chapter 1: The Dawn of Digital Currency

In the early 21st century, the world witnessed the birth of a revolutionary concept—digital currency. This new form of money, based on cryptographic principles, promised to change the way we think about finance forever. At its core, digital currency aimed to provide a decentralized, secure, and transparent means of transaction, free from the constraints of traditional banking systems.

Bitcoin, created by the mysterious Satoshi Nakamoto, was the first to capture the public's imagination. It offered a glimpse into a future where individuals could transact directly without the need for intermediaries. The idea of a currency that could exist purely in the digital realm, powered by blockchain technology, sparked a wave of excitement and skepticism alike.

As Bitcoin gained traction, it paved the way for a plethora of other digital currencies. Each of these new entrants brought their unique propositions to the table, from Ethereum's smart contracts to Ripple's focus on facilitating international payments. The landscape of digital currency was rapidly evolving, and the world was just beginning to understand its potential and implications.

However, the journey of digital currency was far from smooth. Regulatory challenges, security concerns, and the volatility of the market posed significant hurdles. But for those who believed in the transformative power of blockchain technology, these obstacles were merely part of the growing pains of a nascent industry.

2

Chapter 2: The Rise of Altcoins

As Bitcoin established its foothold, a myriad of alternative cryptocurrencies, or altcoins, began to emerge. These digital currencies sought to address the limitations of Bitcoin and explore new use cases. Altcoins represented the diverse and dynamic nature of the crypto ecosystem, each with its vision and purpose.

Ethereum, founded by Vitalik Buterin, introduced the concept of smart contracts, programmable agreements that could self-execute when predefined conditions were met. This innovation opened up a world of possibilities, from decentralized applications (DApps) to automated financial services. Ethereum's success inspired a wave of new projects, each striving to push the boundaries of what blockchain technology could achieve.

Litecoin, created by Charlie Lee, aimed to be the "silver" to Bitcoin's "gold." It offered faster transaction times and a different hashing algorithm, making it a popular choice for users seeking quick and efficient transactions. Meanwhile, Ripple focused on revolutionizing cross-border payments, partnering with banks and financial institutions to streamline international money transfers.

The rise of altcoins was not without its challenges. Competition was fierce, and many projects struggled to gain traction or maintain relevance. Scams and fraudulent schemes also plagued the market, tarnishing the reputation of legitimate projects. Despite these setbacks, the altcoin market continued to grow, driven by innovation and the relentless pursuit of a decentralized future.

3

Chapter 3: The Bull Run and the Bubble

The cryptocurrency market experienced its first major bull run in 2017, capturing the attention of mainstream media and investors worldwide. Prices of digital currencies soared to unprecedented heights, creating a frenzy of speculation and investment. Bitcoin reached an all-time high, and countless altcoins followed suit, fueled by a surge of new investors eager to capitalize on the booming market.

However, the rapid rise in prices was not sustainable. As with any speculative bubble, the market was driven by irrational exuberance and hype rather than fundamental value. Many new investors entered the market without fully understanding the technology or the risks involved, leading to a volatile and unpredictable environment.

The inevitable correction came in early 2018, as prices plummeted and the market entered a prolonged bear phase. This crash exposed the vulnerabilities of the crypto market, highlighting issues such as regulatory uncertainty, security breaches, and the lack of real-world adoption. Projects that had relied on hype and speculation struggled to survive, while more robust and innovative projects continued to build and develop.

The lessons learned from the 2017 bull run and subsequent crash were invaluable. Investors and developers alike gained a deeper understanding of the market's dynamics and the importance of due diligence. The crash also underscored the need for greater transparency, regulation, and security within the crypto space, setting the stage for a more mature and resilient market.

4

Chapter 4: Blockchain Beyond Currency

While digital currencies were the most visible application of blockchain technology, they represented just the tip of the iceberg. The underlying technology of blockchain had the potential to revolutionize a wide range of industries, from supply chain management to healthcare.

In the supply chain sector, blockchain offered a way to create transparent and tamper-proof records of goods as they moved through the production and distribution process. This innovation could significantly reduce fraud, increase efficiency, and enhance traceability. Companies like IBM and Walmart began experimenting with blockchain solutions to streamline their supply chains and improve customer trust.

In healthcare, blockchain presented opportunities to secure patient data, streamline medical records, and improve drug traceability. By creating a decentralized and immutable ledger, healthcare providers could ensure the integrity and privacy of patient information while facilitating better coordination of care. Projects like MedRec and PharmaLedger explored these possibilities, demonstrating the potential of blockchain to transform the healthcare landscape.

The potential applications of blockchain extended far beyond these examples. In finance, decentralized finance (DeFi) platforms leveraged blockchain to create open and accessible financial services without the need for traditional intermediaries. In the creative industry, non-fungible tokens (NFTs) enabled artists to tokenize their work, providing new revenue streams and ownership models.

Blockchain's versatility and potential for innovation were clear, but the road to mainstream adoption was fraught with challenges. Scalability, interoperability, and regulatory hurdles needed to be addressed for blockchain to achieve its full potential. As the technology continued to evolve, it became evident that the future of blockchain lay in its ability to integrate seamlessly with existing systems and create tangible value across various sectors.

5

Chapter 5: The Regulatory Landscape

As the popularity of digital currencies grew, so did the attention of regulatory authorities around the world. Governments and financial institutions were faced with the challenge of understanding and addressing this new and rapidly evolving market. The decentralized nature of cryptocurrencies posed a unique challenge, as it defied traditional regulatory frameworks.

In the United States, the Securities and Exchange Commission (SEC) took a keen interest in regulating initial coin offerings (ICOs), which had become a popular method for startups to raise funds. The SEC aimed to protect investors from fraudulent schemes and ensure transparency in the market. Other countries, such as Japan and South Korea, also implemented regulatory measures to oversee the crypto market and prevent illicit activities.

However, not all regulatory approaches were the same. Some countries, like China, took a more stringent stance by banning ICOs and shutting down cryptocurrency exchanges. On the other hand, countries like Switzerland and Malta adopted more crypto-friendly regulations, positioning themselves as hubs for blockchain innovation.

The regulatory landscape was a mixed bag, with some regions embracing digital currencies while others remained cautious or outright hostile. The key challenge for regulators was striking a balance between fostering innovation and protecting consumers. As the industry matured, it became clear that a cooperative approach between regulators and the crypto community was essential for the sustainable growth of digital currencies.

6

Chapter 6: The Role of Institutional Investors

The entry of institutional investors marked a significant milestone in the evolution of the crypto market. While early adopters and retail investors had driven the initial growth, the involvement of large financial institutions brought a new level of legitimacy and stability to the market.

Investment firms, hedge funds, and even traditional banks began to explore the potential of digital assets. Companies like Grayscale and Fidelity launched crypto investment products, providing institutional investors with a safe and regulated way to gain exposure to digital currencies. The influx of institutional capital contributed to the growth and maturity of the market.

Moreover, the development of regulated financial instruments, such as Bitcoin futures and exchange-traded funds (ETFs), further facilitated institutional participation. These products allowed investors to hedge their positions and manage risk more effectively, attracting a broader range of participants to the market.

The role of institutional investors was not limited to financial investment alone. Many institutions also invested in blockchain technology and infrastructure, recognizing its potential to transform various industries. This institutional involvement helped drive innovation and development within the crypto space, paving the way for broader adoption and acceptance.

7

Chapter 7: Decentralized Finance (DeFi) Revolution

Decentralized finance, or DeFi, emerged as one of the most transformative trends within the cryptocurrency space. DeFi aimed to recreate traditional financial systems using blockchain technology, offering decentralized alternatives to banking, lending, trading, and more.

The core principle of DeFi was to eliminate intermediaries and provide open and permissionless access to financial services. Users could borrow, lend, trade, and earn interest on their digital assets without relying on traditional financial institutions. Smart contracts, running on blockchain networks like Ethereum, automated these processes and ensured transparency and security.

DeFi platforms like Uniswap, Compound, and Aave gained widespread popularity, attracting billions of dollars in total value locked (TVL). These platforms enabled users to participate in decentralized trading, yield farming, and liquidity provision, offering attractive returns and new opportunities for financial innovation.

However, the rapid growth of DeFi also brought challenges. The complexity of smart contracts and the nascent nature of the technology made DeFi platforms susceptible to hacks and vulnerabilities. Regulatory scrutiny also increased, as authorities sought to understand and address the risks associated with decentralized financial systems.

Despite these challenges, the DeFi revolution showcased the potential of blockchain technology to disrupt and democratize traditional finance. It highlighted the importance of innovation and security in building a sustainable and inclusive financial ecosystem.

8

Chapter 8: Non-Fungible Tokens (NFTs) and the Creative Economy

Non-fungible tokens, or NFTs, represented a significant breakthrough in the intersection of blockchain technology and the creative economy. Unlike cryptocurrencies, which are fungible and interchangeable, NFTs are unique digital assets that represent ownership of a specific item or piece of content.

NFTs gained mainstream attention through high-profile sales of digital art, music, and collectibles. Artists, musicians, and creators leveraged NFTs to monetize their work directly, bypassing traditional intermediaries and retaining greater control over their intellectual property. Platforms like OpenSea, Rarible, and Foundation became popular marketplaces for buying, selling, and trading NFTs.

The creative potential of NFTs extended beyond digital art. Virtual real estate, in-game assets, and even virtual fashion items were tokenized and sold as NFTs. This opened up new avenues for creators to engage with their audiences and explore innovative business models.

The rise of NFTs also sparked debates about their environmental impact, given the energy-intensive nature of blockchain networks like Ethereum. Efforts to transition to more sustainable blockchain solutions, such as Ethereum 2.0 and layer 2 scaling solutions, aimed to address these concerns and ensure the long-term viability of the NFT market.

NFTs demonstrated the versatility of blockchain technology and its potential to revolutionize the creative economy. They empowered creators and collectors alike, fostering a new era of digital ownership and innovation.

9

Chapter 9: Security and the Fight Against Fraud

As the digital currency market grew, so did the importance of security. The decentralized nature of cryptocurrencies meant that users were responsible for safeguarding their assets, leading to a heightened focus on cybersecurity and fraud prevention.

Hacks and security breaches became a significant concern, with high-profile incidents such as the Mt. Gox hack highlighting the vulnerabilities of cryptocurrency exchanges. These events underscored the need for robust security measures, both at the individual and institutional levels.

To combat these threats, developers and security experts worked tirelessly to enhance the security of blockchain networks. Techniques such as multi-signature wallets, hardware wallets, and cold storage solutions provided users with more secure ways to store their digital assets. Additionally, advancements in encryption and cryptographic algorithms further strengthened the integrity of blockchain systems.

Regulatory authorities also played a crucial role in the fight against fraud and money laundering. Know Your Customer (KYC) and Anti-Money Laundering (AML) regulations were implemented to ensure that exchanges and financial institutions could verify the identities of their users and monitor suspicious activities. These measures aimed to create a safer and more transparent environment for digital currency transactions.

Despite these efforts, security remained an ongoing challenge. As technology evolved, so did the tactics of malicious actors. The crypto community continued to prioritize security innovations and education, recognizing that the fight against fraud required constant vigilance and adaptation.

10

Chapter 10: The Global Impact of Digital Currency

Digital currencies had a profound impact on the global economy, transcending borders and providing financial opportunities to people around the world. In regions with unstable currencies or limited access to traditional banking services, cryptocurrencies offered a lifeline.

In countries facing economic crises, such as Venezuela and Zimbabwe, digital currencies became a means of preserving wealth and accessing global markets. The decentralized nature of cryptocurrencies allowed individuals to bypass government restrictions and hyperinflation, providing a level of financial stability that was otherwise unattainable.

Cryptocurrencies also played a significant role in remittances, enabling faster and cheaper cross-border money transfers. Traditional remittance services often involved high fees and lengthy processing times, but digital currencies provided an efficient and cost-effective alternative. This had a positive impact on migrant workers and their families, who relied on remittances as a source of income.

The global adoption of digital currencies also spurred innovation and entrepreneurship. Blockchain startups and projects emerged in every corner of the world, contributing to the growth of a vibrant and diverse ecosystem.

This global collaboration fostered a culture of innovation, with developers and entrepreneurs working together to address local challenges and create solutions with global relevance.

However, the global impact of digital currencies was not without its challenges. Regulatory differences, technological barriers, and the digital divide posed significant obstacles to widespread adoption. The crypto community continued to work towards creating inclusive and accessible solutions that could empower individuals and communities worldwide.

11

Chapter 11: The Future of Digital Currency

As we look to the future, the potential of digital currencies remains vast and largely untapped. The ongoing development of blockchain technology, coupled with increasing awareness and adoption, suggests that digital currencies will continue to evolve and play a significant role in the global financial landscape.

One key area of growth is the integration of digital currencies with traditional financial systems. Central Bank Digital Currencies (CBDCs) are being explored by governments around the world as a way to harness the benefits of digital currency while maintaining monetary stability and control. CBDCs could provide a bridge between the traditional and digital financial systems, offering the advantages of blockchain technology within a regulated framework.

Interoperability and scalability are also critical factors for the future success of digital currencies. Efforts to enhance the performance and compatibility of blockchain networks are ongoing, with projects like Polkadot and Cosmos working towards creating interconnected ecosystems. These advancements could unlock new possibilities for cross-chain transactions and applications, further expanding the reach and utility of digital currencies.

Moreover, the continued growth of decentralized finance (DeFi) and non-fungible tokens (NFTs) hints at a future where blockchain technology is integrated into various aspects of everyday life. From financial services to entertainment, digital currencies and blockchain applications are poised to reshape industries and create new opportunities.

While the future is uncertain, the resilience and innovation of the crypto community suggest that digital currencies will remain a dynamic and influential force. As technology advances and the regulatory landscape evolves, the world of digital currency will continue to push the boundaries of what is possible.

12

Chapter 12: Embracing the Crypto Wave

The journey through the highs and lows of digital currency has been nothing short of exhilarating. From the early days of Bitcoin to the rise of altcoins, DeFi, and NFTs, the crypto landscape has been marked by innovation, challenges, and transformative potential.

For individuals and businesses looking to embrace the crypto wave, the key lies in education and responsible participation. Understanding the technology, staying informed about market trends, and practicing good security hygiene are essential steps for navigating the dynamic world of digital currencies.

As the crypto ecosystem continues to evolve, so too will the opportunities and challenges it presents. By staying curious, adaptable, and open-minded, individuals and businesses can harness the potential of digital currencies to drive innovation, foster financial inclusion, and create positive change.

In the end, the story of digital currency is one of human ingenuity and the relentless pursuit of a better future. It is a testament to the power of technology to disrupt and transform, and to the resilience of a global community united by a shared vision of decentralization and empowerment.

So, whether you're a seasoned crypto enthusiast or just beginning your journey, remember that the waves of digital currency are ever-changing. Embrace the ride, stay informed, and continue exploring the limitless possibilities of this exciting new frontier.

www.ingramcontent.com/pod-product-compliance
Lightning Source LLC
LaVergne TN
LVHW020508080526
838202LV00057B/6233